Poems of a Not.   .n Lace-Runner

Five Leaves Bookshop Occasional Papers

Available from Five Leaves or other bookshops worldwide. Papers marked * not currently available. UK P&P inc. if ordered direct from Five Leaves Bookshop.

www.fiveleavesbookshop.co.uk

Poems of a Nottingham Lace-Runner
Mary Bailey

Introduction by John Goodridge

Five Leaves Bookshop Occasional Papers

Poems of a Nottingham Lace-Runner
Mary Bailey

Edited with an introduction by John Goodridge

First published in 1826

This edition published in 2022
by Five Leaves Bookshop
14a Long Row, Nottingham NG1 2DH
www.fiveleavesbookshop.co.uk

Five Leaves Bookshop Occasional Paper 18
ISBN: 978-1-915434-00-5

Designed and typeset by Five Leaves Bookshop

Printed in Great Britain

Contents

Introduction

John Goodridge

Mary Bailey (1775?-1828), of Sneinton, Nottingham, seems a unique figure, a lone female voice in the predominantly masculine world of early Nottingham working-class poetry. She bears witness in her verses to the conditions of women's labour, and though not the first to do so, offers significant and specific perspectives on this. She worked in domestic service 'as a ladies' maid in a family of rank and title', according to her obituary (reproduced as an appendix, below), and took on the relentlessly hard work of bringing up a large number of children, some eight or nine of whom survived. She did so presumably with little assistance from her sickly tailor husband, whose 'delicate health' following her death 'precludes the labour necessary for their maintenance'. A line in her poem 'To the Ladies' tells us that she also dealt in 'all kinds of old and cast-off clothes'. But her main paid occupation was that of a lace-runner, a woman who embroidered lace designs onto a base net. Lacemaking was a principal industry in Nottingham in her time. Lace-running was skilled, immensely demanding, and sheer hard work and, as we learn from her poems, tough on the eyesight as well as the fingers, and poorly recompensed.

Although there are only thirteen poems in the slim pamphlet here reprinted, they cover a lot of ground. From the outset she is concerned above all with the middle-class women who were her primary patrons and potential readers — see the predominantly female subscribers' list at the end of the volume for evidence of that — as well as being the main purchasers of the embroidered lace that she created. Excusing any deficiencies of the verse in a prose note, 'To the Reader', followed by 'To the Critics', which pleads that she must feed her children and notes how she has been encouraged by the 'favourable opinion' of 'some ladies', she continues the volume with two dramatically contrasted images of these middle-class 'ladies' who so influenced her life.

'To a Lady who visited the author when she was in great distress' is a song of gratitude to a woman who has helped to relieve her sufferings at a moment of crisis. Charitable work was one of the few non-domestic activities open to respectable middle-class women, and Bailey's gratitude to this woman recognises the value of an intervention of this sort. The charitable lady's dark twin is the subject of the poem that follows, 'To a Lady who desired me to pray for the death of my youngest child'. Middle-class moralising about how many children poor people should or should not have is still with us today, unfortunately: indeed it is enshrined in government welfare policies, and has lost nothing of its moral hypocrisy and repugnance. Bailey's natural delight in her children, the care and concern she shows for them, clearly evident in this poem and poems such as 'The Author to Her Infant Twins', offers a powerful response to the spiteful death-wish-by-proxy of this second 'Lady'. But it comes at a cost for, as the poem reflects, she must needs agonise over her own feelings in order to rebuff it.

Having addressed these two dramatic polarities of middle-class female 'charitable' attitudes towards her as a working-class woman, the supportive and the judgmental, Mary Bailey is now ready to address her own profession as a lace-runner, and make her case for supporting her better in this to the 'ladies', in her poem, 'Petition to the British Fair'. The phrase simply means British women but manages to imply other things too: ideas of

'British' justice and freedom, perhaps, 'fair' play, 'fair' behaviour, even a 'fair' appearance in the faces of her ladies. This appeal is central to her whole project, so she has to pitch it just right, and makes her title do a lot of the work for her. She has other strategies, too. The poem has the attractive bouncing rhythm of a waltz-time song (her poems are often song-like): the refrain 'The RUNNERS of NOTTINGHAM LACE' gives a nice rolling triple-syllable based rhythm. She uses humour, and a key image is a partly parodic one of fine ladies at their looking-glass, making themselves beautiful with the 'lily white veil' that keeps both male 'gazers' and the sun at bay, or a 'lace dress' that 'fair Venus' herself would love. She sets this cleverly against the runners who have made these beautiful things, and surely deserve fair reward. The appeal is artfully put: the ladies' 'kind exertions' may 'soften our fate', so that the caps and veils they make can more effectively be the full focus of the runners' efforts. A further 'Address to the Ladies' turns from lace-running to her work of poetry, to appeal for their support in this area too.

Mary Bailey's other poems afford us varied glimpses of her life: the memory of a holy man; a holiday; an artless verse-letter; several poems written to an occasion. One of the most interesting is certainly 'The Locust'. It tells of an unusual confrontation in which the speaker's moral values override the social deference of class. The speaker recalls how she saw two middle-class girls tormenting a locust, pinning it and taking pleasure in its agonies. She berates them for this cruelty:

> For shame! let it go, then I eagerly cried:
>   Can you be so cruel as this?
> And look at your bonnets and pretty white frocks,
>   And, remember, at school you're call'd Miss.

> To a nice school you go, where a lady doth teach,
>> And you much finer feelings should learn;
> But, I'm better than you, though my frock's common blue,
>> While my heart doth such cruelty spurn.

She appeals to their class, gender and educational status: as middle-class girls they should know better, and by condoning cruelty they are betraying an education that should have taught them morality and compassion, and to be girls of 'finer feelings'. There is also a child-adult dynamic at play, and they reply angrily (but in equally class-conscious terms) that it is none of her business, and she had 'no right' even to approach them. They see the locust as property which they may use as they wish, with no sense of there being a moral issue. But she ignores this, snatches the tormented insect from them, ignoring their loud 'bellows', and destroys it, 'because it could not get well'. It is an extraordinarily dramatic moment, when the class, gender and ethical tensions present in her poetry suddenly explode into violent action. Even her awareness of clothing as a marker of status, the 'common blue' of her frock, will not hold her back from asserting her moral conviction that she is 'better than' these well-dressed but perverse children, with whom she deals very directly, and without fear or hesitation. And underlining the moral purpose of this tale, the anti-cruelty message, the poem is addressed to two other young girls:

> Dear Sally and Ann, I've a sad tale to tell;
>> I'm sure you'll be grieved when you hear:
> This moment my heart with sorrow doth swell,
>> And I scarce can help shedding a tear.

The poem ends with her showing the two addressee girls the dead locust: here it is.

It is important to bring Mary Bailey's poems back into circulation. Her verses show us a sensibility little-known in histories of the period, a poor woman using the power of verse to express a sense of her place in the world, her negotations with others, and the pleasures and hardships of her life. She breaks up the male monopoly in Nottingham working-class poetry, and gives a vital insight into the world of female labour that was so widespread and important in the city during those years.

John Goodridge
Nottingham Trent University

I am grateful to Nottingham Local Studies Library, and to Dr Dawn Whatman, whose work alerted me to the existence of these poems.

TO THE READER

The writer of the following Verses does not presume to send them to the world as perfect Poetry: she is conscious that they are very deficient; but, as some Ladies have been pleased to express a favourable opinion of them, she has been encouraged to commit them to the press, hoping that, what is not correct, will meet with an excuse from the candid reader.

TO THE CRITICS

May it please the ALMIGHTY on my distress to look,
And send His blessing with my little book;
And screen it from the CRITIC's piercing eye,
Which might at once my labours all destroy:
Should they find fault, which is, alas! too common,
They'd only set their wit against a Woman!
Against my composition should they rail,
And of this little Treasure spoil the sale,—
'Tis not the *chaff*, divested of the grain,
That for their time I'd wish them to obtain;
But for their labour very little gains,
And eight small Children to reward their pains:
This do I wish, and wish it from my soul—
And make them feed and clothe and mind the whole!

MARY BAILEY

TO A LADY

WHO VISITED THE AUTHOR WHEN SHE WAS IN GREAT DISTRESS

The night was dark, and damp, and cold,
    And summer's sun was o'er,
When ladies to the fire creep,
    And shut the parlour door.

Not such the lady of my theme,
    Fair virtue's greatest proof;
She left her comfortable hearth,
    And sought my humble roof:

No damps nor darkness did she fear,
    Nor hesitating stand;
She knew that poverty was here,
    And keen affliction's hand.

The day and evening hard I work'd,
    In sickness, and in pain,
In hopes, for my dear little babes,
    Some fire and bread to gain.

The clock went eight—my work was done,
    Away, in haste I fled;
Nor had I then the slightest doubt,
    But soon to obtain some bread:

But disappointment mock'd my hopes,—
    Back, pennyless, I came:
'Tis only you, can sympathize,
    Who've known and felt the same.

With uprais'd eyes to Heaven, I cried—
    O God! how hard's my lot;
Nor was a prison dreaded more
    Than entering my cot.

Each infant eye on me was fix'd;
    With woe my utterance fled,
While all the four, at once, did lisp—
    Pray, mother, where's the bread?

My heart was full, I could not speak,
    With grief my eyes ran o'er;
But, ere I could petition Heaven,
    A rap was at my door.

Heaven knows our wants before we ask;
    This was His wise decree;
He look'd below—saw none more fit,
    His messenger to be.

Then entered in my much-lov'd friend,
    My great distress to share,
And on her arm a basket held,
    Which pride would blush to bear.

With looks so placid, meek, and mild,
    She set the burden down:
Plenty and novelty at once
    My empty board did crown.

To replenish next my fireless grate,
    Her ready purse she drew;
And inward satisfaction felt,
    Which misers never knew.

Ye Powers above! watch o'er the maid,
    All scarcity controul;
Pour down your plenty in her lap,
    Nor bind her generous soul.

Fate often breaks the bosom's cord,—
    That nature's finest string:
Just such this lady's heart was form'd
    And oft that heart's been wrong'd.

May keen remorse my slumbers break,
    If I'm so base and rude
To wound her gen'rous, feeling heart
    With vile ingratitude.

If half her goodness I rehearse,
    Or half her favours tell,
My little, poor, imperfect verse
    Must to a volume swell.

TO A LADY

WHO DESIRED ME TO PRAY FOR THE DEATH OF MY YOUNGEST CHILD

Fair lady, when you me advis'd,
　　To pray Heaven my baby to take,
I acquainted the Muse, and she could not refuse,
　　But send you a line for its sake.

She thought it was hard for the poor little bairn,
　　Who had always good humour display'd;
And not for a moment, though much put about,
　　The least discontent had betray'd.

The great Author who sent it below,
　　Will take care that 'tis clothed and fed:
How hard I should think its death-blow,
　　For wanting a morsel of bread.

Though entirely destitute I,
　　Or e'en cast in a desert so wild,
Shall I dare to presumptuously cry—
　　O! take from my bosom my child?

No.—For the dear babe at my breast,
　　Each storm I'll so willingly weather:
Her innocent smile shall my troubles beguile,
And make poverty light as a feather.

Her dear little prattling tongue
    Will soon my attention engage:
She's a comfort to me now she's young;
    And may be the support of my age.

'Tis a boon our Creator has lent,
    And 'tis right if he call it away:
Be it taken or spar'd I'm content;
    But ne'er for its death can I pray.

Then, lady, forbear to advise,
    Till a mother's affections you feel;
Then you'll own that to wound is unkind,
    Where none have the power to heal.

PETITION
TO THE BRITISH FAIR

You ladies of Britain, we most humbly address,
    And hope you will take it in hand,
And at once condescend on poor RUNNERS to think,
    When dress'd at your glasses you stand.

How little you think of that lily-white veil
    That shields you from gazers and sun;
How hard have we work'd, and our eyes how we've strain'd,
    When those beautiful flowers we run.

O view the ball-room, where beauty beams round,
    And shines with such elegant grace,
And think are you no ways indebted to us,
    The RUNNERS of NOTTINGHAM LACE.

The dress that a Queen or a Duchess becomes,
    To us, owes its beauty, in part:
Then think of us, pray, in your elegant homes,
    For we copy both nature and art.

If fair Venus could come from the skies,
    And had ne'er seen a lace dress before,
She would deem it, with joy and surprize,
    The most beautiful robe that is wore.

How pleasant's the task, whenever we're ask'd,
　　To work hard to beautify you;
Then I'm sure you will own, with candour, unmask'd,
　　Good food and good clothing's our due;

But the price is so low, that, sad to relate,
　　We cannot these blessings obtain;
But your kind exertions may soften our fate,
　　And, if not, we content must remain.

Now, should fortune prove kind, how hard will we strive,
　　Our kind interceders to deck
With caps for the head, and veils for the face,
　　And collars and frills for the neck.

May the quickest invention come forth,
　　Each beautiful feature to grace;
Yours, humbly, ourselves we devote—
　　The RUNNERS of NOTTINGHAM LACE.

ON THE

DEATH OF THE REV. DR. WYLDE,

LATE OF NOTTINGHAM

Dare I presume, with unaccustom'd pen,
To tell the virtues of the best of men!
But can the Muse behold this loss, severe,
And neither drop a line nor shed a tear,
To him who gain'd such general respect?
No! gratitude forbids the gross neglect!
If none more able to write, the task be mine
To celebrate this eminent Divine.—
Mild was the season, through the rolling year,
Scarce had we felt a night of frost, severe,
Till that most hapless night that ever froze—
The sad foundation of our present woes!
Ah! to our town, how dreadful was the stroke
Of that sad morn on which his limb was broke?
Thousands will point to the spot, and, sighing, tell
The slippery steps on which the Doctor fell!
Still, for awhile, with us he did remain;
His christian fortitude surmounting pain.
Prospects on high, his pious bosom fill:
He bows submissive to his Maker's will.
Ah! Could his people's tears and wishes save,
And snatch their Guardian from the envied grave!
We had not had the pain to say—he's dead;
And o'er his grave our fruitless sorrows shed.
With ready hand he succour'd the distress'd;
Virtue supported, and all vice suppress'd.
To him the injured wife ne'er sued in vain:

He call'd the erring husband back again;—
Show'd him the path in which the virtuous trod:
And turned the vilest sinner to his God!
As husband, father, pastor, justice, friend,
Him few could equal, none on earth transcend.
Sheep of his flock, repeat the mournful lay!
For fifty years you bore his holy sway.
How many hundred times your walls have rung
With the effectual blessings from his tongue.
From him the promises were doubly sweet;
From him the threats convey'd a double weight.
Long, long he preach'd to you redeeming grace.
And fill'd with holy awe, the sacred place.
God grant that none may ever leave the fold;
That all, in bliss, their Shepherd may behold.

ADDRESS
TO THE LADIES

Most honoured Ladies, at your feet I lay
    My poor, imperfect Muse;
Trusting, you'll some attention pay,
    And these few lines peruse.

As thrives the shrub beneath the lofty pine,
    And grows secure beside its stately form;
Fears not the sun, at day's meridian tide,
    And stands, unhurt, amidst the lashing storm:

So I, and my dear little family,
    May, by your condescension, gain support;
Screen'd from the storms of keen adversity,
    Beneath the smile of opulence and worth.

For you, whose bosoms are from scorn exempt,
    Will not despise my lowly occupation,
Nor treat my humble errand with contempt,
    Nor yet discourage this my speculation.

But lest I should upon your time intrude,
    This verse, the business of my paper, shews,
(Hoping you will not think me pert or rude,)
    I buy all kinds of old and cast-off clothes.

Upon your goodness I will ne'er intrude:
    A fair and honest price I wish to give,
Then, from your favours, pray, don't me exclude;
    I only want a profit just to live.

And, to those ladies who've encouraged me,
    My heartfelt thanks, sincerely, I return;
Hoping their favours will continued be,
    And with warm gratitude my heart shall burn.

ODE TO HOPE

When drear misfortune crowds each prospect here,
    And gives to every painful feeling birth;
What is it then my drooping heart can cheer,
    And is my only solace upon the earth?—

                  'Tis Hope.

Though keen affliction scarce a day omits,
    But pays continual visits to my home;
What my weak shoulders to the burden fits,
    And, flatt'ring, whispers better days to come?—

                  'Tis Hope.

When poverty's sharp arrows pierce my soul,
    And bid me rapid to destruction fly;
What, instantly the rashest thoughts controul,
    And bid me on her promises rely?—

                  'Tis Hope.

And still deluded on from year to year,
    I fondly to the soft deceiver cleave;
And oft she stops my sighs and dries my tears;
    Though she but flatter, yet, I still believe—

                  False Hope.

Trust her not, then, calm reason seems to say,
    Her promis'd favours are so seldom given;
And when they are, they're fleeting as the day;
    But rather wish to see her crown'd in Heaven;—

                  Sweet Hope.

MARY BAILEY

LINES,

WRITTEN IN JULY, ON WIDOW HIND'S GARDEN, AT HINTS, IN STAFFORDSHIRE

Hail! my sweet garden, on the hill,
  Where every tint is found;
Where fragrant fields the prospect fill,
  And woods are scattered round.

My cottage neat—my home's complete,
  Though I've no wealth in store:
A moss-rose through my window peeps—
  A fig-tree guards my door.

These flowers, that now around them throw
  Their sweet perfuming breath,
How much, in winter, do they show
  Their much-loved master's death.

One blighted rose, that can't disclose
  Its beauties to the sun,
Is just an emblem of my woes,
  Since thy dear course was run.

One female friend who knows my grief,
  And strives to soothe my lot,
Oft leaves the hurry of the town
  To share my rural cot.

Too soon, alas! her visits end,
    And I am left alone:
My children, dear, are distant plac'd,
    And thou for ever gone.

Over my disconsolate breast
    Have roll'd two tedious years;
And many a tree, thy hand has set,
    I've watered with my tears.

'Twas God's great will—I must submit,
    That gave a shorter date;
He'll call me hence, when he thinks fit,
    To share thy blessed state.

Submissive, then, I humbly wait
    Till death shall set me free,
And I exchange this flow'ry mount
    For paradise and thee!

POETIC LETTER

Dear brother and sister the packet is come
To let you both know we are safely got home:
And, in this epistle, I'm happy to say—
My dear little Ellinor slept all the way.
If more of my baby you wish me to tell,
I'm glad to inform you, she's now pretty well.
Bailey gives his kind love, and bids me to say—
He shall come down to see you on next Christmas day,
If things should roll smooth, and the weather allow,
And nothing more happens than we know of now.
In love to you both, my dear children do join,
With thanks for your pudding, your ham, and your wine.
I hope you'll write frequent, and we'll not neglect:—
We subscribe ourselves yours, with the greatest respect.

THE LOCUST

Dear Sally and Ann, I've a sad tale to tell;
    I'm sure you'll be grieved when you hear:
This moment my heart with sorrow doth swell,
    And I scarce can help shedding a tear.

Just now, of an errand, you know I have run;
    And as I through the Market-place came,
I heard a young lady exclaim—what nice fun:
    Pray, Eliza, do you like the game?

Very much, said Eliza, 'tis better, I'm sure,
    Than running about till we're hot;
For the heat, love, you know, is so hard to endure;
    And I'm glad this plaything we've got.

But what was the sight, that did so much delight;
    Dear sisters, I tremble to tell;—
'Twas a poor little locust, pierc'd through with a pin,
    That into their cruel hands fell.

The agonies keen, the poor insect did feel,
    The young ladies did highly delight,
While quick it turn'd round on the sad galling pin,
And the thread it endeavour'd to bite.

For shame! let it go, then I eagerly cried:
    Can you be so cruel as this?
And look at your bonnets and pretty white frocks,
    And, remember, at school you're call'd Miss.

To a nice school you go, where a lady doth teach,
    And you much finer feelings should learn;
But, I'm better than you, though my frock's common blue,
    While my heart doth such cruelty spurn.

'Tis no business of yours, both at once, they exclaim'd,
    And near us you'd no right to come:
We shall do as we please, you may rest quite assur'd,
    And, therefore, I beg you'll get home.

Then I snatch'd the poor locust, I'm happy to tell,
    Tho' loudly indeed they did bellow:
I kill'd it because it could not get well;
    And this is the poor little fellow.

LINES

ON THE DEATH OF A GENTLEMAN OF BASFORD

He's gone!—the patient sufferer's gone to rest,
    And every storm is o'er:
He's safely number'd with the blest
    On Canaan's happy shore.

Long, with true Christian fortitude, he bore
    The chast'ning scourge of the Almighty's hand:—
Ceas'd has the conflict, and the storm is o'er,
    And, lo! he joins the sweet, angelic band!

When his dear relatives crowded round his bed,
    And heav'd, with inward grief, the pensive sigh;
Mourn not for me, the patient suff'rer said,
    My peace is made—I'm well prepar'd to die.

When pious friends the sacred anthem rais'd,
    With feeble pulse, he strove to swell the song;
Strain'd every nerve to sing his Saviour's praise,
    As fell the Hallelujahs from his tongue.

O! may we all, like him, be well prepar'd;
    Like him, be found among the pure in heart,
Willing to linger—if 'tis God's command;
    Or, summon'd—like him, ready to depart.

Thy wife and daughter, dear—those bosom friends.
　　Who, with such kind attention, watch'd thy side:
Far as thy Heavenly power to earth extends,
　　Be still thy widow's—be thy orphan's guide.

Guard them, thro' life's rough road, to realms of bliss:
　　And if affliction's bread must be their food,
Grant that, like thee, the chast'ning rod they kiss;
　　Give them thy spirit, and thy fortitude.

Deep in the gloomy grave! thy mortal frame
　　Is doom'd to moulder with its kindred dust!
But that ethereal spark of Heavenly flame
　　Gains the reward of all its hopes and trust.

LINES

WRITTEN TO A GENTLEMAN WHO ASKED THE AUTHOR TO WRITE
SOME VERSES ON A YOUNG LADY, BUT WHO AFTERWARDS ALTERED
HIS MIND

One day a poor woman I saw,
 As musing she walk'd on the road,
And into our shop she just happen'd to pop,
 And a copy of verses she show'd.

I smiled, for you know I admire the art,
 And some little attention I paid;
And both father and I condescended to read
 The verses this rhymer had made.

Mean elf as I was, for I can't but reflect;
 Why what in the world should I do,
But, forgetting to pay you a proper respect,
 I ask'd her to write upon you.

As a father afflicted you left,
 I knew you had anguish forlorn;
Of one parent already bereft;
 And in grief from the other was torn.

If Homer or Virgil I'd summon'd to write;
 Or Milton have rais'd from the dead;
Or could but have call'd forth a Byron or White
 To have written, dear Miss, in her stead.

Why then I am sure, you'd have pardon'd the thought,
    An would even have read with delight;
But now you'll forgive, as no further 'tis brought,
    For I did not permit her to write.

THE AUTHOR TO HER INFANT TWINS

Welcome, dear little strangers, welcome here,
    Altho' to keen adversity you're come,
Hope's matchless balm each dreary hour shall cheer,
    And shed her comforts o'er our wretched home.

God can dispel the gloom that hovers round,
    And loose us from the grasp of poverty;
For, in the midst of judgment, mercy's found,
    And will be shown, I humbly trust, to me:

Remove her iron hand that spoils each joy,
    And robs the parent of all earthly bliss.
When I, with rapture, press my girl and boy,
    Her frozen looks chill every warming kiss.

I hope kind Heaven will our sorrows view,
    And look with pity on this harmless pair;
And tho' its heavy judgments are our due,
    Let not these tender little infants share.

But sleep, my babes, I'll not disturb your rest;
    Ah! sleep secure, beneath the Heavenly powers:
I'll think the present troubles for the best;
    He yet can strew this thorny path with flowers.

Subscribers' Names

Lady Parkyns,
Ruddington
Miss Youle,
Nottingham
Mrs. Boothby,
Standard Hill
Miss Turner
Miss Shaw
Miss Greaves,
Nottingham
Mrs. Enfield
Mrs. Wilson
Mrs. Taylor
Miss Maria Taylor
Mrs. Carpenter
Mrs. Wylde
Mrs. Wilkins
A Friend, 2 copies
Dr. Davidson
Mrs. Davidson
Mr. Warburton
Miss Boultbee
Miss E. Boultbee
Miss Pritt
Mr. T. Pritt
Miss Davidson
Mrs. Sherbrooke Gell
Mrs. Gilbert
Mrs. Nicholson
Miss Sharpe
Miss Thompson
Miss Flint
Miss Wood
Mrs. Hall
Miss Trueman

Mr. Nunn
Mrs. Chatteries
Mrs. Dyson
Miss A. Nuttall
Mrs. I. Gibson
Mrs. Hazard
Mr. Preston
Mrs. Leeson
Mrs. Warner
Mrs. Grisenthwaite
Miss Wilson
Miss Fisher
Mrs. Roworth
Mrs. Smith
Mrs. Smith, *Radford*
Mrs. Clarke
Miss Chambers
Mr. Brown
Mr. Worth
Mrs. Harrison
Mr. Hulse
Miss Mills
Mr. T. Ward
Mrs. Taylor
Mrs. Glover
Miss Smith
Mrs. Cooper
Miss Cooper
Miss A. Cooper
Mr. Brown
Mr. Danks
Mrs. Earnshaw
Miss Cooper, *Hoton*, 2 c.
Miss Rowland, do.
Mrs. Jackson, *Burton*, 2

Mrs. Etherington
Mrs. Sharp
Mrs. I. Harrison
Mrs. Lacey
Mr. Green
Miss Gee
Mrs. Simpson
Miss Owencroft
Mrs. Morley
Mr. Cheetham
Mr. Parnham
Mrs. Skipwith
Mrs. Minster
Mrs. Orme
Miss Potts
Mr. Sansom
Mr. Streeton
Mr. Watts
Mr. Toplis
Mr. Howitt
Mrs. Coppock
Mr. Godfrey
Miss Townsend
Mr. Marlow
Mr. Telley

Appendix: Mary Bailey's obituary

On Sunday evening, Mrs. Mary Bailey, wife of Mr. Bailey, tailor, New Charles-Street, Nottingham. Among "the short and simple annals of the poor," we know of few individuals who have greater claims to the sympathy of the opulent, than the object of this memoir could show. She had evidently received an education superior to the rank of life in which she latterly moved, and her conversation afforded ample evidence of her claims; she had been ladies' maid in a family of rank and title. Some months ago she published a small pamphlet of poems, in order to procure her some assistance in supporting a sick husband and a numerous family of helpless children; and she met with encouragement from many respectable ladies in Nottingham, who commiserated her abject condition. The first and last verse of a poem addressed to her twin infants, born about fifteen months since, are as follows... [quotes from 'The Author to Her Infant Twins'] ...About six weeks ago she was confined of her *ninth* surviving child; in a fortnight after she was sufficiently recovered to go out, when being employed to write a letter (which she was in the habit of doing for females of inferior attainments) she took cold; an inflammation fixed on her lungs, she was too poor to employ medical assistance, and her benefactors were not aware of her situation till too late. On Wednesday her remains were followed to the grave by her husband, and their nine children, the eldest of whom is not thirteen, and the three youngest were carried in the arms of sympathising neighbours. We hope that the relief which was afforded to the mother by the bountiful, will not be withheld from the destitute children, whose father's delicate health precludes the labour necessary for their maintenance.

('Died', *Nottingham Review and General Advertiser for the Midland Counties*, Friday 29 August 1828, p. 3.)

Notes

There are two editions of her book (see 'Further Reading', below), both dated 1826, both published in Nottingham, but by separate publishers: C. N. Wright, and Samuel Bennett. The Bennett printing is marked on the title page as 'Second Edition', and does appear to have gone through a process of revision and improvement. This is the copy text used in the present edition, though I have referred to both.

On the Death of the Revd. Dr. Wylde, of Nottingham
Revd. Charles Wylde (1748-1825), D.D., Vicar of Waltham, in Lincoln, Prebendary of Southwell official of the Archdeacon of Nottingham and Rector of St. Nicholas in Nottingham for 52 years until his death in 1825.

Lines, Written in July, on Widow Hind's garden, at Hints, in Staffordshire
'Bailey appears in this poem as "a female friend" and this work reveals her capacity to depict a scene (rural or urban) through its inhabitants. The garden represents the widow's lost family, providing comfort.' (Whatman). Edlin-White notes that the poem refers to Virgil, Milton, Byron and Henry Kirke White. Hints is near Tamworth.

Subscribers' Names
There are 90 subscribers, 68 identifiably female, 21 identifiably male, and apparently all local people. 'Mr Howitt' may have been either Richard or William Howitt, brothers who were both, along with William's wife Mary, major supporters of local writers in this period.

Lady Parkyns

Charlotte Mary Parkyns (1801-1838), née Smith, later Tyser, was the eldest daughter of George and Eliza Margaret Smith of Edwalton. In 1820 she married Sir Thomas Boultbee Parkyns (1797-1833), the 5th Baronet of Bunny Park. She was the mother of the famous explorer Mansfield Parkyns (1823-1884). After her husband died in 1833, she re-married, to Henry Tyser, esq., M.D., of Stamford-hill, on 23 September 1835 (*Gents. Mag.*, n.s. 3 (1835), 85). The Parkyns family were 'well-known in local affairs', and left a local legacy in the present-day name of Parkyns Street, Ruddington. She appears to be a key figure, and it is possible that Mary Bailey worked for her during her time in service.

Further Reading

Mary Bailey

Bailey, Mary, *Poems, Humourous and Sentimental, by Mary Bailey, Kingston Place, Nottingham* (Nottingham: C. N. Wright, 1826); second edition (Nottingham: Samuel Bennett, 1826); original copies of both are held in the Local Studies Collection, Nottingham Libraries, albeit in fragile condition. No other copies are known.

Bailey, Mary, (obituary), *Nottingham Review and General Advertiser for the Midland Counties*, Friday 29 August 1828, p. 3 (reproduced above, Appendix).

'Lost Poet of the Industrial Age', *Nottingham Post*, 27 June 2013.

Whatman, Dawn Carol, 'Mary Bailey, Poverty and the Lace Trade', in 'Recovering British Labouring-class Women Poets, 1780-1837', PhD dissertation, Nottingham Trent University, 2018.

Nottingham Working-class Poets

Baird, John, *Follow the Moon and Stars: a literary journey through Nottinghamshire* (Nottingham: Five Leaves, 2021).

Binfield, Kevin (ed.), *Writings of the Luddites* (Baltimore: Johns Hopkins University Press, 2004).

Collins, Philip, 'Thomas Cooper the Chartist: Byron and the "Poets of the Poor"', Nottingham Byron Lectures 1969, https://www.nottingham.ac.uk/research/groups/crlc/docu ments/foundationlectures/collins.pdf [accessed 22/07/22]

Edlin-White, Rowena, *Exploring Nottinghamshire Writers* (Nottingham: Five Leaves, 2017).

Hall, Spencer T., *Biographical Sketches of Remarkable People, Chiefly from Personal Recollection* (London, 1873), via Google Books: see especially p. 298 ff.

Early Working-class Women Poets

Boos, Florence S. (ed.), *Working-Class Women Poets in Victorian Britain* (Peterborough, Ontario: Broadview Press, 2008).

Goodridge, John, 'A Catalogue of British and Irish Labouring-Class and Self-Taught Poets, c. 1700-1900', online at www.academia.edu and Humanities Commons (the 278 female poets are marked [F] and may be browsed by searching for this).

Goodridge, John, and others (eds), *Eighteenth-Century Labouring-Class Poets and Nineteenth Century Labouring-Class Poets* (London: Pickering & Chatto, 2003 and 2006), six volumes, including selections from 23 working-class women poets.

Landry, Donna, *The Muses of Resistance: Laboring-Class Women's Poetry in Britain 1739-1796* (Cambridge: Cambridge University Press, 1990).

Index of Titles and First Lines

Also available from Five Leaves

Follow the Moon and Stars: a literary journey through Nottinghamshire *by John Baird*
2021, 480 pages, colour photos throughout,
hardback 9781910170908, £25, paperback 9781910170892, £14.99

St Anns, The Final Chapter *by Peter Richardson*
2021, 122 pages, 98 B&W/colour photos
hardback 9781910170861, £30, paperback 9781910170854, £20

St Anns, The End of an Era *by Peter Richardson*
2020, 116 pages, 96 B&W/colour photos
hardback 9781910170793, £30, paperback 9781910170786, £20

Viking Nottinghamshire *by Rebecca Gregory*
2017, 310 pages, colour photos throughout, 9781910170359, £12.99

Exploring Nottinghamshire Writers *by Rowena Edlin-White*
2017, 310 pages, colour photos throughout, 9781910170359, £12.99

These Seven *by 7 Nottingham authors, ed. Ross Bradshaw*
2015, 136 pages, 12 B&W illustrations, 9781910170205, £3.00

Look Back in Anger: The Miners' Strike in Nottinghamshire 30 Years On *by Harry Paterson*
2014, 298 pages, B&W & colour photos, 9781907869952, £9.99

The Open Door *by Alan Sillitoe*
2012, 354 pages, 9781907869631, £12.99

Made in Nottingham: A Writer's Return *by Peter Mortimer*
2012, 242 pages, 9781907869525, £9.99

Available from Five Leaves or other bookshops worldwide. UK P&P inc.
if ordered direct from Five Leaves Bookshop.

www.fiveleavesbookshop.co.uk